WORLD BANK STAFF WORKING PAPERS
Number 626

Some Temporal Aspects of Development
A Survey

R. S. Eckaus

The World Bank
Washington, D.C., U.S.A.

This is a working document published informally by the World Bank. To present the results of research with the least possible delay, the typescript has not been prepared in accordance with the procedures appropriate to formal printed texts, and the World Bank accepts no responsibility for errors. The publication is supplied at a token charge to defray part of the cost of manufacture and distribution.

The World Bank does not accept responsibility for the views expressed herein, which are those of the authors and should not be attributed to the World Bank or to its affiliated organizations. The findings, interpretations, and conclusions are the results of research supported by the Bank; they do not necessarily represent official policy of the Bank. The designations employed, the presentation of material, and any maps used in this document are solely for the convenience of the reader and do not imply the expression of any opinion whatsoever on the part of the World Bank or its affiliates concerning the legal status of any country, territory, city, area, or of its authorities, or concerning the delimitation of its boundaries, or national affiliation.

The full range of World Bank publications, both free and for sale, is described in the *Catalog of Publications*; the continuing research program is outlined in *Abstracts of Current Studies*. Both booklets are updated annually; the most recent edition of each is available without charge from the Publications Sales Unit, Department T, The World Bank, 1818 H Street, N.W., Washington, D.C. 20433, U.S.A., or from the European Office of the Bank, 66 avenue d'Iéna, 75116 Paris, France.

R. S. Eckaus, in the Department of Economics, Massachusetts Institute of Technology, is a consultant to the World Bank.

Library of Congress Cataloging in Publication Data

Eckaus, Richard S., 1926–
    Some temporal aspects of development.

    (World Bank staff working papers ; no. 626)
    Bibliography: p.
    1. Economic development. 2. Time and economic
reactions. I. Title. II. Series.
HD82.E245 1983   338.9   83–25959
ISBN 0–8213–0300–7

ABSTRACT

Development has proved a relatively slow process.
This paper is a preliminary attempt to identify and
explain factors that contribute to the temporal dimension
of development. These factors include well-known
gestation lags on investment, but also the temporal
processes in improving labor supplies in the creation of
"modern labor force", market organization and efficiency,
government support functions, and capital productivity.

The analysis focuses on identifying practical reasons
that some processes take a long time to accomplish, and on
specifying precedence sequences that require certain
processes to be accomplished before others can effectively
begin. This then helps explain the factors which could
lengthen the development process.

The objective of this paper is not to provide hard
quantitative data on the temporal lags, but to identify
major sources of lags and to stimulate thinking on how they
might be quantified, and more importantly, of how they might
be reduced.

ACKNOWLEDGEMENT

This paper was prepared for the World Bank, which,
however, bears no responsibility for its contents. The
author appreciates the opportunity to consider the issues
and is particularly grateful to Mr. John Shilling who
both presented and discussed the topics. The timely and
very competent assistance of Mr. Joe Klesner of the
Department of Political Science at M.I.T. is acknowledged.

EXTRACTO

El desarrollo ha resultado ser un proceso relativamente lento. Este documento es un intento preliminar por identificar y explicar algunos factores que contribuyen a la dimensión temporal del desarrollo. Estos factores incluyen las consabidas demoras de gestación de las inversiones, pero también comprenden los procesos temporales para mejorar la oferta de mano de obra con miras a la creación de una "fuerza laboral moderna", la organización y eficacia de los mercados, las funciones de apoyo gubernamentales y la productividad del capital.

El análisis se centra en la identificación de las razones prácticas por las que algunos procesos toman largo tiempo, y también en la determinación de las secuencias de precedencia que exigen que ciertos procesos se realicen antes de que otros puedan de hecho comenzar. Esto ayuda a explicar los factores que podrían prolongar el proceso de desarrollo.

El objetivo de este trabajo no es proporcionar datos cuantitativos sólidos sobre las demoras temporales, sino más bien identificar las causas principales de demoras y estimular la reflexión acerca de cómo podrían cuantificarse y, lo que es más importante, de cómo podrían reducirse.

Le développement se révèle être un processus relativement lent. Cet ouvrage tente de recenser et d'expliquer les facteurs qui lui donnent sa dimension temporelle. Ces facteurs sont non seulement les décalages bien connus dus à la gestation des investissements, mais aussi les délais nécessaires pour former la main-d'oeuvre dont une économie moderne a besoin et améliorer l'organisation et l'efficacité du marché, la contribution de l'Etat et la productivité du capital.

L'analyse vise en particulier à déterminer les raisons pratiques pour lesquelles certains processus mettent longtemps à s'accomplir et à préciser la chronologie de tous ces processus, les uns devant nécessairement précéder les autres. Il est alors plus facile d'expliquer les facteurs qui pourraient ralentir le processus de développement.

L'objet de ce document n'est pas de fournir des données quantitatives précises sur les décalages temporels mais d'expliquer quelles en sont généralement les causes et d'inciter le lecteur à se demander comment elles pourraient être quantifiées et, chose plus importante, comment elles pourraient être éliminées dans une certaine mesure.

TABLE OF CONTENTS

I. Introduction

This essay deals with a neglected aspect of economic development: the length of the temporal processes or sequences which are involved. Such neglect is surprising, and it may be denied, because the temporal dimensions of the economic and social changes required by development would seem to be at the heart of the subject.[1] Yet the conditions which make simultaneity of efforts and results impossible and, thus, retard growth have, in fact, not been explored in detail.

It is true that change and, particularly, growth have been dealt with extensively in the development literature, but most often in a manner which avoids explicit consideration of time sequences, lags and delays. While the avoidance may, in part, be due to the analytic difficulties associated with an explicit consideration of time processes, those difficulties are not the major obstacle. That seems to be the lack of organized and explicit empirical information. Everyone knows that, for a lot of reasons, it takes time to develop, but no one knows much about the time sequences. Or, at least, little information has been collected and studied which isolates and measures them. This state of affairs may, reflexively, be due to a lack of appreciation of their importance, but it will be argued below that the data desired are, in principle, difficult to acquire. As a result there have been few empirical characterizations on which the kind of applied theory practiced in development economics might be based. In any case, even now an essay on the subject of temporal processes in development must, of necessity, be speculative in nature. The reader will, therefore, find repeated use of the subjunctive tense, references to "general knowledge" and "folklore" and apologies for inadequate evidence.

"Temporal processes in development" are those which are related in an essential manner to the passage of time. "Essential" in this usage means that the neglect or putting aside of such features will lead to important mistakes in assessing the characteristics of development and the formation of policy. Economic growth theory certainly embodies some of the essential aspects of temporal processes. It omits many other features of development intrinsically associated with the passage of time. Moreover, its focus on steady-state or asymptotic conditions has limited its usefulness in development policy, which is nearly always concerned with non-steady state and non-asymptotic conditions. Except for some time sequences which are closely related to engineering practices and for which engineering judgements have often been accepted, the relevant lags and delays are seldom considered even in the practical analysis of projects and programs.

Most of development assistance policy is preoccupied with processes of adjustment which take place through time to achieve future goals of resource allocation and output, relative prices, income distribution and other economic features. The time required for projects and programs to reach their objectives is a critical determinant of the character and potential sources of financing. If the processes of development were quick and easy, development assistance could be managed from a tent city and development assistance budgets could be regarded as temporary. The fact that the World Bank is conducted as if it were, for all practical purposes, a permanent organization reveals the prevailing view of the correct time horizon for development. That is, however, based more on the lessons of experience than on theoretical understanding tested with facts.

In surveying the subject of time sequences in development, the first step will be to review a bit of methodology which will help in thinking about the issues. That will facilitate a more detailed consideration of the various sources and types of temporal processes. The first to be considered will be those associated with labor supply. Changes over time in social and political structures and behavior which directly affect economic development will be taken up next. Temporal processes associated with market organization and functioning and capital formation will then be discussed. Some suggestions for policy which arise from the analysis will be considered in the concluding section.

II. Thinking about temporal development sequences

Since changes over time are at the heart of development, it would be expected that they would have a major role in development theory. That is true, in some important ways, and hardly true at all in other important ways. The distinctions emerge clearly in the treatment of capital formation. In the Harrod-Domar model, perhaps the simplest and still most widely used economic growth theory, when formulated in discrete time units, the relations are:

(1) $Y = bK$,

where Y is GNP; b, the output-capital ratio, and K, capital stock. So,

(2) $\Delta Y = b\Delta K = b \cdot I$ or $I = \Delta Y/b$

where ΔY is, say, the annual change in GNP; ΔK is the annual change in capital stock which is identified with I, investment. Since

(3) $S = s \cdot Y$,

where S is annual savings, and s is the average savings rate out of GNP and savings = investment, in equilibrium,

(4) $s\,Y = \Delta Y/b$ or $\Delta Y/Y = sb$

The model certainly deals with temporal processes, as it generates a growth rate, but, putting aside its unrealistic "knife-edge stability" qualities, it conceals the time processes involved. Those are revealed by writing out equation (2) in full:

$$(5) \quad Y(t) - Y(t-1) = b \, I(t-1)$$

That is, investment in period (t-1) is assumed to result in capacity in period (t), which is used in the same period to produce additional output. There is just one period lag between the use of resources to form new capital and the production of output by that capital. This single gestation lag is the only time sequence recognized by the model. In fact, the activities which are called capital formation or investment must cumulate over a series of time periods, in manner determined by technology and economic behavioral influences, in order to create capital with the capacity to produce output.

A graph which is useful in depicting the temporal processes involved in the formation and use of capacity, and which will be helpful later in considering other types of temporal processes, is presented in Figure 1. The horizontal axi is assumed to represent the life of a particular project. Measured vertically upward are the inputs into that project and vertically downward, the stream of outputs from the project.

Starting at 0, the beginning of year 1, there are a series of inputs in eac year before output begins, which are clearly investment inputs. Investment continues up to and including year 4 during which some output first appears, for which current inputs are also required. By the end of year 4, the investment process is over. In years 10 and 15, major maintenance is carried out with increased input requirements. After year 20, the flow of inputs is reduced as the plant is gradually phased out of production.

The growth of output from the project's operation is gradual, accelerating at first and then growing at a lower rate with temporary reductions due to the major maintenance projects which interfere with production. The trend increase in output during most of the project's lifetime has been explained in several ways: the adjustment and improved coordination of plant and equipment, growing

Figure 1

Example of Time Profile of Project Inputs and Outputs

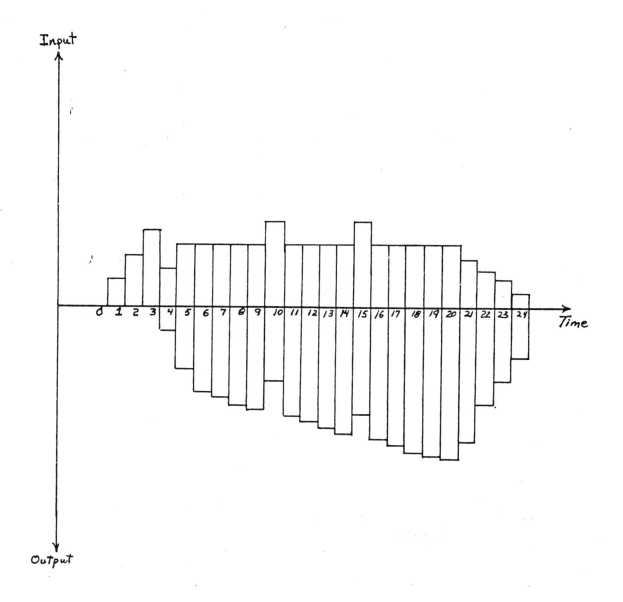

experience in using the plant, increasing skill of the labor force and, perhaps, continuing technical improvements in the plant and materials. The picture makes the distinction between investment and the capacity to produce clear. It also suggests the importance of the scheduling of investment and the relation of that scheduling to the other activities which contribute to output. There may or may not be alternatives in the scheduling which create important choices or trade-offs in costs and returns.

Construction of a single plant is a discontinuous process with a clear time sequence. Such sequences would be hidden if aggregate growth were at a steady rate and only total inputs and outputs were observed. In fact, there might appear to be a virtual simultaneity. But the temporal relations would still be determining the amount of investment which would have to be carried out in each period in order to maintain the constant proportional additions to the capital stock and to available productive capacity in each year.

The example may be used to illustrate five temporal sequences which are related to capacity creation and use and which will have analogies in other temporal processes: gestation, maturation, learning-by-doing, maintenance and depreciation. The first is, perhaps, most familiar. Before capacity can become available, there must be a period of time during which the actual work is carried out. That is, the "gestation" period. The time may be lengthened or shortened depending on the resources but there are usually technical limits to both types of adjustment. Within those technical limits there will be economic choices which trade off inputs against the time required for project completion.

After the project is completed, more time is typically required for "maturation." This is the experience with operations which is necessary for the project to achieve the output levels for which it was designed. There are also economic choices with respect to this sequence. Use of more experienced labor, for example, can reduce the time necessary to bring the plant and labor force to rated productivities.

Learning-by-doing is another distinct time process. It has been identified as the improvement in output, associated with increasing productivity of the labor force, due to accumulated experience over the lifetime of the project. Learning-by-doing is one reason why it is difficult to define "capacity" as the upper limit to output because that limit may itself grow with experience. Perhaps there are economic trade-offs in this time process also, but what actually happens in the course of the changes remains somewhat mysterious.[2]

With a little imagination one might also perceive in the figure the temporal sequences associated with depreciation and the effects of maintenance. In this example, the latter is somewhat disruptive of production while it is being carried out. Intertemporal substitutions of inputs and output may be achieved if depreciation is related to the rate of output rather than the passage of time, by the use of particular levels of raw materials, and by the acceleration or delaying of maintenance. The possibilities have relatively ignored in the economic literature though they are practically important.[3]

Intertemporal substitution possibilities in production have been described above in terms of discrete time. Each process adds a lag, which may be expanded or reduced. The discreteness makes it easier to distinguish the separate processes. However, the same influences can be described in terms of continuous time. Again the Harrod-Domar model can be used to exemplify the time processes. The conventional model, using the same notation as above with the time dimensions of variables being altered appropriately for continuous time, is:

$$(6) \qquad dK/dt = I = S = sY$$

$$(7) \qquad \frac{dY}{dt} = \frac{1}{10} \frac{dK}{dt} = \frac{1}{b} (sY)$$

$$(8) \qquad \frac{\frac{dY}{dt}}{Y} = \frac{s}{b}$$

In this version investment is identical to increases in capacity production. If, however, production capacity, Z, depends on the cumulation of investment over some period of time, T, then

$$(9) \qquad Z = \int_{0}^{T} I \, d(t)$$

This version is still too simple, as it stands, as it suggests that it is the accumulated investment over a period of time which is important, no matter when the investment occurs within the period. Yet the timing of investment is significant and the alternative time patterns of inputs and outputs are subject to technical constraints as well as managerial decisions.

There are inherent technological delays in the relations between inputs and output in investment and current production are inherent in production activity. While, as noted, it is often possible to lengthen or shorten the delays, with corresponding changes in the total inputs applied, and the timing as well as quantity of output, there will be limits to some temporal adjustments. A twenty-year-old bottle of port wine requires just twenty years to age. But a small building can be constructed more or less quickly depending on the amount of manpower and other resources simultaneously employed. A multistory building must wait for the first nineteen floors to be built before the twentieth floor can be completed. Even if the delays in building each floor are reduced by increasing the resources employed, there will still be a substantial lag in reaching the twentieth floor.

Learning requires time, whether it is formal and takes place in classrooms, or is on-the-job training. Not all of the reasons for the time requirements for classroom education are well understood, but the reality is certainly widely appreciated. There is less known about on-the-job training, in fact there is startlingly little known. To the extent that it is a function of experience, that ties the process to production rates.[4]

Many individual adjustments to changes in the economic and social environment in the course of development, but which cannot realistically be called learning or education, also require time to accomplish. For those economists who call "human capital formation" anything which involves benefit to the personal qualities or conditions of individuals, all such adjustments could be recognized as analogous to lags in physical capital formation. For example, occupational changes, even when spatial migration is not involved, require periods of adjustment. Those may not be learning periods in the sense of creation of job skills but of learning different work pacings, different roles in the work team, different means of communication and so on. Working with a heterogeneous team is often a major personal adjustment which takes time to accomplish successfully.

Social adjustment processes, including political changes, which affect economic activity have their own time sequences, for example, the implementation of governmental functions. It is transparently not the case that the goals and paths of adjustment which satisfy a social welfare function are instantly perceived and acted upon in the most effective manner by all participants. Information about methods and alternatives and even the formulation of rules for improving social welfare often require experience which clarifies the consequences of particular actions. Social decision-making is to some degree a process of trial and error, of iteration through time.

By endowing each of these temporal processes with sufficiently comprehensive connotations, for example, including biological changes in "technological" delays, the categorization becomes comprehensive. Practically, the different sources of temporal delays in the functions may not be identified separately. For example, some gestation and maturation delays may have their origins in technology and some in individual and social adjustment processes. The discussion which follows will be organized primarily by resources and functions, as above, rather than by attempting to isolate the fundamental sources of particular time sequences. That is partly because those fundamental sources are seldom understood and, in any case, it will often be necessary to focus policy on particular production inputs and economic functions.

III. Temporal processes in labor supply.

Development requires changes in the proportions of the labor force employed in the various sectors of the economy, which means geographic as well as industrial and occupational shifts of labor. New patterns of social behavior must be learned in movements from the countryside to urban areas and from, say, street vending to factory employment. There will be different sources and kinds of authority exercised. New work relationships must be adopted. Recruitment and migration, changes in socialization on-the-job and off-the-job and job training are all involved, each with its own time configurations. Intuition suggests that there may well be relations of substitution and complementarity among the time sequences in these functions and the technologies and sectors in which labor of various types is used. There is little specific known about these time sequences or about the trade-offs among them, although the general view is that the processes are "slow".[5]

A strong example may help in suggesting the potential significance of the time delays in the expansion of labor supply to growing sectors in developing countries. Consider the creation of labor skills, as if that were a capital formation process as in Figure 1 above. "Inputs" must take place over a period of time after which there are increases in productivity. The time "delays" are necessary for formal and vocational education and on-the-job training and job experience. In the United States, according to the U.S. Dictionary of Occupational Titles, for many jobs the formal education needed is simply literacy and numeracy and the job-training and experience required is a few months or less, so the "delays" are relatively short. However, in order to be a supervisor in many types of work, a college education and up to four years of experience are required. To be a chief executive requires another 4 to 10 years.[6]

Suppose these estimates are taken literally and it also is assumed that there is no way of substituting for chief executives with committees or fully computerized operations research and information flow systems. Then, starting from a situation in which no one has enough experience to be the president of a large organization, there would have to be as much as a 10 year lag before anyone had enough practical knowledge to bring an establishment to its potential productivity.

Ten years is a long lag indeed and some people would think it too short. The rarity of chief executive officers who take their positions at age 32, ten years out of college, may be due to queuing in line and the absence of real competition for jobs. But, in most institutions even more than ten years experience is regarded as necessary for the most senior positions. Even if allowance is made for the self-serving exaggeration of senior executives whose opinions have been solicited, this "experience lag" is longer than the longest gestation period which has been suggested for physical capital formation. Suppose also that useful experience is gained more slowly in developing countries than in the U.S. where large scale business organizations with many good administrators are common. Then the experience lag may stretch out even longer.[7] Moreover, it is not a once-and-for-all time delay after which, with careful programming, fully qualified executives could become available exactly as needed. There are delays in recruitment and imprecise or non-existent scheduling and bottlenecks in the opportunities for acquiring experience which will be continuing constraints on the creation of a cadre of effective managers. A detailed calculation is not necessary to suggest that the length of time required to relax this particular limitation could be quite a long one.

The time delays in labor supply processes have not been considered in any depth either by the "manpower" or "human capital" approaches to labor force analysis. The former has, dealt mainly with formal training "requirements" for different types of occupations and the latter has not been concerned with the issue at all, except in so far as the delays have had an effect on the timing of the, "returns to investment in human capital." As will be pointed out, labor force sociology has also not explicitly dealt with temporal issues, so there is little, if any, organized research on which to base quantitative assessments.

Recruitment of a labor supply to new or growing industries in developing industries will often, perhaps typically, involve not only spatial migration but also a movement from one work culture to another.[8] It is reasonable to suppose that this makes the process more time consuming. While there may be some persons who leap at the chance to change their work and life styles, the more conventional view is that such movements are a slow response to economic and other social incentives after watching the experience of others who have made the move. Moreover, the folklore is full of stories of persons who have clung to the "old ways" and never made the transition to the style of modernized labor supply. Thus, to some extent, as with "experience", successful recruitment and migration depends on previous successful development, but successful development experience requires successful recruitment and migration.

These arguments may appear to be both obvious and pointless in the face of the reality of large scale, rural-urban population movements and the rapid growth of urban areas in developing countries. Yet the rural-urban movement is not a tidal wave everywhere and even where it rolls apace, there is evidence that there may be delays in the permanent commitment of labor to particular industrial sectors in urban areas. In addition, the growing evidence about the composition of migrating labor suggests that a large proportion of the persons who move out of rural areas are among the less well-educated and the less qualified, at least in some countries. So the problems of recruitment of relatively qualified persons may, to some extent, co-exist with the reality of the waves of rural-urban migration.

There are, of course, factors which facilitate labor force adjustments. In particular, both self-selection and employer selection processes make it easier to recruit a vigorous and qualified labor force at each stage of the modernization of labor supply. Individuals dissatisfied with their status and aggressively trying to improve themselves, and talented persons frustrated in traditional roles which do not make use of their talents may, "self-recruit," into new jobs.[9] Employers choosing out of a large "reserve army of unemployed" are more likely to find the persons more physically and intellectually adept and adaptable to new labor conditions than when choosing from a smaller pool. Unfortunately, we can only tell the possible stories and there is no data, at least nothing systematic on any scale, which would permit the quantification of the phenomena.

If one believes the current migration models, the delays in the migration process may be quite important. If not, once the calculation of relative advantages is made, the appropriate number of persons should pack their belongings and move. Migration would then stop until some further change created a differential which migration would again eliminate. Perhaps that is really the way the world works and it is only a continuous change in the data of the calculations which is responsible for the continuing movement. It is also plausible that migration is a slow adjustment to calculated incentives. As another alternative, potential migrants move just when their calculations tell them they should, but the results of the calculations vary among individuals, due to differences in their fixed and variable costs of the migration, as well as possible differences in benefits. So what is observed as a slow adjustment to the economic incentives for migration, may really be quick adjustments by different individuals for whom the calculated benefits and costs change over time.

Yet this last story seems implausible and the suspicion remains that there are time delays in the response by individuals and families to the incentives to migrate. It is mainly in modernized societies, characterized by a relatively high degree of individualism, that decisions such as those involved in migration are made on personal grounds. More typically, and especially in developing countries, it is to be expected that migration decisions involve the extended family even, possibly, an entire village, tribe or local caste. That is in part because there are perceived individual obligations to these larger groups. In addition, through urban connections, the larger groups can facilitate the migration process and there will also be potential benefits to the larger groups through claims on any individual rewards to migration.[10] The resolution of conflicting appraisals of benefits and costs and their apportionment requires time: committees can be expected to work no more quickly in villages than in boardrooms.

Unless one believes in perfect capital markets which can be used to finance the "human capital" creation through migration, then accumulation through personal saving of the funds necessary will also require time. While there may well be accumulations in the extended family or village, presumably they have been dedicated to other purposes than migration before that becomes a "profitable" alternative. Without good financial markets the reallocation of those funds will not be quick.

Turning to education, as another process in adapting the labor force to development, there appears to be rough agreement with respect to the time periods required to educate individuals to the different levels of academic achievement, recognizing that the same academic degree may represent different levels of competence. What is still less clear are the relations among levels of academic competence and economic performance. Even in those professions for which there are more or less conventional standards with respect to formal education, e.g. engineering and medicine, it is known that there are substitution possibilities among persons with different levels of formal and specialized education and, therefore, different time requirements. Yet, there is little quantitative information about those substitution possibilities and how far they can be pushed. The significance of the different proportions of conventional doctors and engineers, practitioners and foremen for the quality of performance of the desired services and overall productivity remains a matter of speculation. Moreover, the relations of substitution and complimentarity among formal education, vocational education and experience are also hardly understood, at least at the level of educational and development planning. Whether those relations are well understood in the hospital, on the plant floor, in the shipping room or office, is, again, not known. For example, the U.S. Census of Population lists workers without college educations performing the functions of engineers. Are they doing less well than college trained engineers? Is on-the-job experience substituting for lack of formal education or are they especially talented?[11] The twenty-five years or so of intensive research by economists on the economics of education has simply not produced useful results on such important questions.

These expressions of uncertainty about some of the most significant aspects of education do not detract from recognition of its fundamental importance as well as the relatively long periods of time involved in educational sequences. One of these functions of education, now coming to be more widely recognized, is that of screening. Education, itself, serves to identify persons who are more or less qualified for different economic roles. The educational process also screens for its own functions by helping to find those persons who will be relatively successful in the various branches of education and more advanced study. Since it is necessary to educate in some stages, partly in order to determine who is to educate in other stages, that lengthens the lags in the process of generating trained persons.

With respect to the role of experience in creating productivity, there is not much more specific which can be said. Like education, experience performs a screening function as well as creating expertise. A good deal of knowledge used in business, administration, as well as all other social activities, is empirical and even specialized to particular situations: "What works for one person, may not for another," etc. Experience also is a means of determining aptitudes which cannot be fully described and measured but which are nonetheless important in coordination and management. The conventional training times and experience requirements in the U.S. and other developed countries reflect both real maturation, union rules and seniority practices designed to control job access Corresponding information for developing countries does not appear to exist.[12]

IV. <u>Sociological influences and lags in the creation of a modernized labor</u>
<u>force</u>

Factor productivity, investment and other contributions to growth depend not
only on what goes on inside individual heads, <u>ceteris paribus</u>, but what goes on,
<u>mutatis mutandis</u>. "Everything else" which is changing includes social patterns
of family and larger scale organization. For better or worse, these economic
transformations and the concomitant modifications in social organizations and
processes go under the headline of "modernization" in the sociological
literature. However, just as the economic development literature, for the most
part, avoids dealing with temporal sequences, so also does the literature on
social change and modernization. Perhaps the latter literature does better by
pointing out where one might look for data on time processes, if one were so
inclined. That empirical studies do not exist is undoubtedly due to the same
intractability that forestalls economic studies of the time dimension of economic
processes, rather than simple oversight. Thus the sociological literature on
development will not yield numbers, but it does provide another important
perspective.

Labor force modernization involves the use of new recruits from the
traditional societies of agriculture and/or handicrafts. For most of these new
workers there will be abrupt changes in their self-images and their social roles
which can be expected to profoundly affect their productivity. The recruitment
of a factory labor force is characteristically accompanied by a differentiation
of functions that were formerly associated in the traditional agricultural,
handicraft and cottage industry systems. In the latter systems family and other
kinship ties are not so wholly separate from work and income as they are with
respect to factory labor recruited and employed on a meritocratic basis.
Ownership of real property or its rental may be associated with other social

roles in traditional systems and may or may not exclude active labor. Rules for association of individuals, lines of authority and the character of authority can all be expected to be different between traditional and modern sectors.

The functional differentiations associated with a modernized labor force in turn require new means for integrating individuals into the society of their workplace, their living places and social interactions. That occurs, in part, within the factory itself, as part of the organizational structure and functioning of the factory. That is not to imply that it is instantly effective, even when the nature of the technology or product seems to demand a particular and unique structure. An assembly line, for example, implies a different set of social relationships and lines of authority and incentives than work in labor teams. The peer group pressure of work gangs, the authority of the foreman or supervisor, the identification with a particular employer, the tax collector, the public school system, the local health service, are all integrating mechanisms. They never perform with complete success the social roles which they assume; neither did the traditional integrative mechanisms.[13]

An important difference between traditional and modern methods of social integration is that the latter more often require explicit monetary transactions either in markets or through taxes and subsidies. In traditional societies, by comparison, the resources required for the services associated with the integrating functions are more often exchanged without recourse to either market transactions or monetary taxes, although traditional monetary payments are also known.

Time is also required for the formation of institutions which integrate workers effectively into a modernized labor force and, thus, maintain or increase labor productivity. For example, if women are to participate in a modernized labor force on a large scale, replacements must be found for the family-kinship institutions which performed child care functions. Day-care centers are one answer but they have their own set of problems and lags which, in turn, affect the productivity of working women.

There is, again, no more than a set of stories or parts of stories which provide hints as to the length and significance of these "sociological" lags. It has been argued, for example, that part of the relative effectiveness of Taiwanese industrialization is due to the location of much of it in close proximity to the home villages of the labor force. That has reduced the disruption of the traditional society and the requirements for new means of integrating the labor force to a modernized society outside of the factory. In turn, it is suggested, the costs of social services to support the labor force have been lower and labor productivity higher than would otherwise have been the case. The use of migratory labor, which is housed in dormitories, for work in mines and factories may also be a way of preserving the social structure of the worker's home villages and of avoiding some costs and time delays in creating new social integrating mechanisms. These are two examples of the preservation and use of aspects of the traditional society to facilitate modernization of production. Examples of replacement of traditional structures and functions with modern elements abound, but, again, there is little organized information about the associated time processes and costs.[14]

One economic function which is closely related to social structure, and which received a great deal of attention in the development literature of the 1950's and 1960's, is entrepreneurial activity. With a few exceptions that attention has virtually vanished from current development discussion for both good reasons and for bad. The question was originally posed in the form, "Is there evidence of entrepreneurial activity in developing countries?" It was answered strongly positively in one study after another. The answers were, perhaps, misleadingly reassuring. Entrepreneurial research has diminished sharply, yet there remain questions as to the circumstances in which entrepreneurial impulses can become effective in the sectors and on the scale necessary for modern development. Vigorous entrepreneurship in a village market does not ensure that opportunities in petrochemicals or cement-making will be recognized and exploited when they emerge. The conclusion that there are, typically, many entrepreneurs who will take advantages of opportunities which exist in a traditional setting does not guarantee that there will be individuals who can play an analogous role - and will be allowed and supported in doing so - in non-traditional settings.[15]

The emergence of entrepreneurs is generally regarded as a sociological phenomenon, time is required if they are to be modern and skilled in ability to handle large scale operations. How much time? That can be expected to differ from society to society and depends on the nature of the educational system as well as the social system. There are no quantitative data. The intuitive concerns of the early investigators in the field probably embodied more than a grain of truth. The fact that entrepreneurial talent in modern sectors and on a modern scale existed in India and Nigeria in the 1950's does not demonstrate that there is no bottleneck of this sort anywhere. Time and social change will still be required to overcome the constraint.

V. Temporal lags in market organization and efficiency

There are economists who find market calculations and market-like transactions everywhere, including in some apparently unlikely personal activities. Yet, there is a sound tradition and much scholarly opinion which holds that, for most of society, there are important social functions which are mediated through nonmarket interactions. It does seem that the scope of market interactions is expanding in developed countries, with an occasional set-back

from the income tax laws and

"do-it-yourself" innovations. In most developing countries the expansion of the

scope of market mediated transactions is one of the major forces of development.

But such expansion does not, in itself, guarantee that markets are working to

produce efficient allocations of resources and use of goods and services,

although, this is accepted, almost as an article of faith, by some economists.

Again there is little organized information with which to enter the

discussion. Casual empiricism, based on a general knowledge of history and

anthropology, suggests that markets for goods develop, and, perhaps, become

reasonably efficient, before markets for productive resources. Large scale

production for national and international trade has, in some instances, been

based on traditional types of mediation of exchanges of resources in plantation

and sharecropping systems. So it cannot be argued that good resource markets are

required for such production. The, Penny Capitalism, described by Sol Tax, and

used by T. Schultz to demonstrate the pervasiveness of market rationality, was a

capitalism of goods markets.[16] Tax explicitly pointed out that the sale of land

was culturally inhibited and there was little said about labor markets.

Goods markets in the traditional sectors of developing countries seldom fit

the rigorous requirements of pure competition, not only because there are

monopolistic elements but because there are differential degrees of participation

in the markets. A significant example may be also found in a non-traditional

sector in the problems which newly industrializing countries have encountered in

"penetrating" international markets. Korea and Taiwan, China relied on Japanese

trading firms to facilitate such penetration at early stages of their industrial

expansion. By comparison, the current active collaboration of many U.S. firms

with those of the newly industrializing countries may explain the relative
success of the latter in entering U.S. markets.

If international markets are costly and time-consuming to "penetrate," even
for relatively standardized commodities, it is reasonable to assume that the
spread of national markets within countries also entails important costs and
time periods. How much? Again, there is little or no information. In some
cases, the critical element is the improvement of transportation. That has been
argued in the case of the economic integration of North and South Italy after
Unification. The effect of Northern dominance in Southern markets, it is argued,
handicapped the development of the South. In the United States, one of the most
spectacular expansions of the internal market came after the opening of the Erie
Canal when the grain of the old Northwest Territories entered eastern markets.

Apart from the obvious and powerful effects of transport costs in creating
and expanding markets, societies must change if markets are to expand, in the
sense that there is growing participation by individuals and to larger categories
of goods, services, and assets. That is, in part, the message of the Polanyi
book, The Great Transformation.[17]

How long does the extension of efficient markets take? Presumably there is
no answer which is the same for all societies. Domestic pressures from internal
politics and the competition of indigenous groups and international pressures may
contribute to the speed of modernization and the expansion of effective markets.
The Japanese economic "miracle" did not blossom immediately after the Meiji
Restoration. The year 1905, when the Japanese fleet defeated the Russian navy is
sometimes used to mark the emergence of a modern Japan. Yet it may well be that
a country can organize a modern military establishment before it can create a
modernized economy, as the evidence of recent world events may signify.

The time periods required for the spread of markets and the extension of
their scope and functions in the course of development are controversial
questions and have even become somewhat ideological. The issues are akin to
Creationism and Darwinism. Did the present system of pervasive market
transactions in developed countries arrive with man on the sixth day of creation,
although with much lower price levels? Or did the market economy evolve slowly,
with fits and starts? If the latter, then what is the time scale of the
evolutionary process and, from the standpoint of development policy, how can the
process be accelerated and by how much? There has been little study and there
are no good answers for these questions.

VI. Government functions and temporal development processes

Political scientists in the last thirty years or so have explicitly analyzed
political development as a process of modernization which, if not the analogue of
economic development is, at least, a roughly corresponding process. That
must certainly be a welcome extension of political analysis, for the economist's
approach, in the modern theory of public finance, is a rather bloodless set of
stories and theories. The aspects of political development which interest
economists are, of course, related to the use of resources and the supply and
distribution of goods and services.

The economic rationale for government has it providing public goods and
offsetting externalities, either directly, by its own supply, or indirectly,
through taxes, subsidy and regulation as well as, generally, monitoring the
system. The ability of a government to do all this depends on its achieving the
attributes of a 'modernized' system. That in turn requires resources which, if
used successfully, will enable government to perform those functions which even

good markets could not, as well as whatever other functions which might be handled oy markets but are assumed by government.

Governments have existed before anyone ever thought of economic development and political modernization. The specific kind of government required for economic development is certainly not unique in terms of style and methods, judging by the heterogeneity one finds in the world. Yet, for all types of government there are a number of conventionally distinguished political functions, which must be performed in the course of political development. They are: (1) creation of national identity, (2) creation of legitimacy, (3) penetration of society to exercise control, (4) participation by citizens, (5) distribution of benefits.[18] As public functions they are not solely the responsibility of government and different societies will involve non-governmental institutions to different degrees. But a modern government must to some extent perform all of these functions. Moreover, in the course of development the specific content of these functions can be expected to change. For example, the educational systems of colonial countries, it is commonly argued, are lacking in national identity and impose the patterns of the imperial power. The lack of national identity, in turn, is a detriment to development as the motivations and skills which the education conveys are not conducive to the development process. As a result, with independence, the educational systems change.

Some of the political functions of government can be associated directly with its economic functions.[19] In the present context the important point is that time, as well as resources, are required for governments to be able to perform these functions effectively. It is not just a matter of organizing an effective government bureaucracy, although that, itself, is a significant and time consuming task. There is also the necessity to achieve a particular set of

relationships between the government and the citizenry and that, in turn,
requires certain, at least indirect, relationships among the citizenry. The time
required for achievement of the national identity and the legitimacy which
assists government in commanding and allocating resources will, of course, depend
on the individual country circumstances and the intensity of the competition of
local and other social loyalties and authorities with the national government.
While some economic functions of a national government can be performed
efficiently by local or other social entities, other economic functions must be
performed on a national scale if they are to be efficient. The specific economic
functions performed by government will depend in part on each country's
public/private sector roles. In every country, however, there is a minimal set
of government functions which can only be carried out efficiently on a national
scale.[20]

The political development literature seems to be barren of quantitative
estimates - or even qualitative speculation - as to the time required for a
government to achieve effective levels of performance with respect to any of its
functions. The difficulty of generalizing is understandable, considering the
range of different original conditions. But even in country studies, there is
only limited reference to the time dimensions involved.[21] There is some
speculation as to the impact of modern communications techniques in creating
national identity and government legitimacy which help make it possible for
governments to carry out other functions. Again, however, there do not appear to
be any quantitative estimates. There is a general presumption that the time
requirements are, typically, not short, i.e. not a "few" years and more than
"several." Of course, most governments now have a history, but even so there
appears to be a consensus that in a number of developing countries there is ample

scope for progress with respect to these functions and especially with respect to the content they must have for economic development.

Among the insights conveyed by this categorization of government functions is the emphasis on "penetration" of the economy as a dimension separate from, or an aspect of, control. At the extensive margin government is often identified with the politicians and bureaucracy of the capital city and the cities with airports and/or railways. There is an intensive margin along which government affects the workings of such basic social units as the family and tribe. The ability to exercise authority in the rural villages, as well as in the urban slums, to extract resources and deliver services, is a critical feature of political development.[22] It is not the case that such penetration and control is the same for all types of government activity related to economic conditions. For example, by effectively controlling national and, perhaps, regional markets for primary agricultural commodities and some major inputs, governments may set prices and even force deliveries of certain agricultural commodities. Import duties and some excise taxes may be relatively easy to collect. On the other hand, income taxes and land taxes may be difficult if not impossible to impose, depending on the constraints within which the government operates.

The functions which governments must perform for economies to develop require resources. As suggested above, the political constraints within which governments operate affect the manner and degree in which they can acquire the resources.[23] If the style of government is to conscript manpower by sending military patrols into urban neighborhoods and rural villages, "penetration" is accomplished in an authoritarian manner. Development, however, requires participation of the citizenry which is, to an important extent, willing.[24] There are many tasks in modern economic development which require sensitive, individual responsibility and others which need group collaboration.[25] There is no example of a modern, developed economy which operates completely by use of the whip. There is coercion in all societies, from tax collection to traffic control, but on the most obvious evidence, development requires "participation."

An hypothesis suggested by this overview is that the ways of extracting resources and providing services which are most efficient in terms of economic criteria will require a relatively high degree of "penetration" and "participation." For example, a lump sum tax, the least distorting of taxes, requires identifying individuals for assessment and collection. Income taxes require declaration and measurement of incomes. But excise taxes, which are among the most distorting of taxes, require least penetration. The "forcing" of savings through inflation can be managed through centralized monetary controls as can distorting tariffs or overvalued exchange rates.

"Participation" also comes in many forms and, what is acceptable or willing behavior in some societies may be overly coercive and regimented in other societies. So, to some degree, the standards are relative, but every society distinguishes the whip and the gun butt from a willing offer. To the extent that the hypothesis relating efficiency in the exercise of government economic responsibilities and success in political modernization is correct, it implies extension in the delays in the temporal processes which lead to economic efficiency in development.

Governments in many developing countries, through their planning agencies and economic ministries, perform many of the functions which markets perform in other countries. The determination of output levels and composition, of the distribution of labor and other resources, the pricing and sometimes the physical distribution of output are all, to varying degrees, matters of government decision-making in developing countries.

The effective formulation and implementation of economic plans do not emerge from government edicts any more than efficient markets spring full blown from the soil of peasant agriculture. Making plans, in the sense of constructing models of development with some degree of sectoral detail, is the easiest part of what goes under the name of economic planning and implementation. The translation of rather aggregated targets into the myriad details of reality is always a compromise between what may be centrist ambitions and practical limitations of knowledge and capacity at the center. Implementing national economic plans is a matter of information flows and administration of the most complex type. The question of whether central planning is more or less efficient than market processes is beside the point here. Some government planning and plan implementation is always carried out and many countries are committed to giving a major role to such planning. So the present issue is how much time is needed for planning to work reasonably well, admitting that in some countries and in some sectors it does that.

Again there is almost nothing which is known. A literature on "plan failure", which would be analogous to analyses of market failure, almost does not exist. Ideology vastly overwhelms the analysis and the problems of separating achievement in this direction from achievement in other areas of government activity are enormous.

One judgment which can be extracted from the analytical and descriptive literature which does exist is that effective planning and plan implementation is not achieved quickly. No one, partisan critic or partisan supporter, claims that. How long is required for the process to become effective? The time scale seems to be in terms of decades, not years.

VII. Temporal changes in capital productivity

Much of the limited discussion which exists about temporal lags in economic processes has focussed on investment in, and operation of, new projects. In the latter context much of the discussion is about activities which have already been taken up here, e.g., the acquisition of labor skills, maturation processes which involve learning how to use equipment and coordinate separate production and distribution sequences, socialization of the labor force, spread of markets and generating and distributing government-provided services. Treating these issues first and separately has helped in distinguishing them from activities or procedures necessarily related to capital formation. There are also some time processes which are capital-specific however. In discussing these, references will occasionally be made to effects already pointed out because they often become most obvious in the course of capital formation.[26]

The concept of the gestation period for new capital should be enlarged to include a planning phase. That requires a time period whose length is itself a matter of economic choice. It appears to be the case that the more originality which is required in planning a project, the greater the length of preparation time and costs of planning. This is the implicit, if not explicit, rationale given for using or adapting designs from other projects with technologies and other features which are "inappropriate" for the new application. In principle there should be a calculation of the saving of present costs and quicker returns versus higher operating costs later, all properly discounted. Undoubtedly some of those calculations are made but the folklore is full of stories of old blueprints being taken out of files and simply re-titled for new projects.

Apart from planning, gestation times may increase with the rate of overall investment, as capital formation requires a number of supporting services whose capacities are probably not balanced.[27]

"Maturation of capital" is, in part, a learning process by the labor force operating a new plant, but a learning process which is highly specific to the particular circumstances. It includes everything from learning how long it takes to travel to work to learning how much error there is in the readings of a particular gauge or marker. Some types of capital also require a "running-in" period, which is not experimentation to learn the idiosyncrasies of particular pieces of equipment, but a period of adjustment of each of the various parts of the equipment to the other parts. That also may be a matter of choice and design and involve trade-offs of current against future costs. In some cases, for example, more highly automated factories can reduce training times for machine operators, although requiring more highly skilled maintenance workers.

Another type of delay in improvement of capital productivity is associated with economies of scale within and outside of the plant. There is a useful analytic literature on the optimal degree of "over-building" which is the creation of capital whose capacity may initially be partially unutilized but which will provide more than offsetting economies of scale when demand grows.[28] "Traded" goods may be purchased where their costs are lowest, but growth of capital productivity in "non-traded" goods which have economies of scale in their production will depend on the speed with which efficient scale of production is reached. There are a number of important examples: electricity, road and rail transport, and ports and warehouses. The rates at which economies of scale "accrue" differ among sectors. There are also differences in initial capital availabilities and changes in patterns of demand over time. These are issues which preoccupied those development economists who advocated "balanced growth."[29] However, the reasoning above implies that "balanced growth," which also minimizes total factor cost in all sectors, at all times is most likely to be impossible.

Another implication of the reasoning is that the differences between actual and optimal capital productivities are likely to be larger in the early phases of development and for small countries than later in development and for larger countries.

In general any "non-linearities" in demand or supply for goods may be a source of variation in capital and other factor productivity in the course of development. This should be extended to "external economies and diseconomies" as well as fully internalized costs and returns. If this is especially emphasized with respect to capital productivities, it reflects the implicit belief that much capital is specific, not only with respect to the particular product and that capital productivity depends on the scale of its output. Analogues can be found in labor skills as discussed above.

Finally, it should be noted the affects of that delays in labor training, in labor adjustment, in sociological adaptations to economic modernization, in market operations and the effectiveness of government functioning are often all attributed to and focussed on capital productivity. That is understandable as these other conditions will influence capital productivity. For foreign suppliers of funds, the returns to capital are often the critical issue and government agencies and private firms alike are often judged by this standard. The discussion above suggests, and the folklore of development, if not the formal analysis, agrees that the reasons for capital productivity are spread widely through the polity, society, and economy.

Consideration of the lags in achieving the rated capital productivities in new projects also provides the occasion to describe how all the temporal processes which have been discussed have a continuing effect in slowing development rather than being a set of obstacles to be overcome once and for all. There are always new investments to be undertaken in the course of development.

Each new project requires assembling a labor force which has not before worked in the particular location, in the physical arrangements, and probably, with the particular technologies. There is a new set of fellow workers. Managers and engineers are not only new to the working force but they, similarly, find themselves in a somewhat strange environment. The project will produce new kinds of output or new amounts of output which have to find a place in the market. Governments may have to provide new services and feel impelled to impose new taxes or regulations.

There is a question as to whether the lags in adjustment should be any shorter in advanced countries than in countries such as India, Brazil, and Egypt which also have substantial cadres of craftsmen and technicians, professionals and administrators in both private and public sectors. This should be expected for several reasons. First, the composition of output, of technology, of skills and required government services are changing relatively rapidly in developing countries. Second, even in the more advanced of the developing countries, literacy and numeracy rates and proportions of technicians and engineers and experienced administrators in the labor force are low, as compared to advanced countries. Third, the educational patterns which do exist are, in some cases, inherited from a colonial past and unsuited to the requirements of development. Finally, the social and political adjustments involved and extensions of markets are relatively large, simply because the developing countries are still at early or intermediate stages in the processes of modernization.

New industrial investments, new projects in agriculture, urban design and construction, extension of government services and provision of new services, all on a relatively large scale are required in the course of development. These strain existing resource and organizational capacities in all countries which push hard at development. While it might be expected that delays would be reduced in the course of development, even that need not be the case as countries move from one type of industrial emphasis to another.

Conclusions and Policy

It is in the nature of an essay of this sort that there are no "results" which lead clearly to new policies. Yet the survey does, if in no other way but by weight of words, suggest some revisions in the conventional appreciation of development processes and lines of analysis to follow which may lead to somewhat new emphases in policies.

The review of the sources of delays in development processes leads to a better assessment of the significance of those delays. The cautions of experienced economists that development is a long, slow process are not just reactionary attempts to maintain a rationale for dependencia, although such influences may not be absent from all such cautions. There are many reasons for delays which reflect real constraints of technology and social behavior.

Longer delays imply lower factor productivity. Compare, for example, two projects with the same capital output ratios, of 2 to 1, and the same constant output streams for twenty years after completion of investment. Assume the first project has a gestation period of only two years while the second has a gestation period of five years. Then, at a 10 percent discount rate, the first has a present discounted value which is 40 percent larger than the second.

As noted frequently above, there is an almost total lack of explicit measurements of the various lags which exist in factor supply adjustments, in progress in market organization, in governmental administrative capabilities, and so on. That is another reason why policy recommendations which explicitly take the delays into account cannot be suggested with confidence. However, there are some suggestions which do emerge from the preceding discussion.

Industries will vary in their gestation and maturation periods, the
adjustments they impose on labor, their demands for government services and the
ease with which they enter foreign and domestic markets. It is possible that the
temporal processes which are characteristic of particular industries have had an
important role in the "success stories" among developing countries. "Export
promotion", for example, has occurred mainly in "light industries" with
relatively short gestation periods, low skill requirements, standardized markets
and limited demands for government services, e.g., textiles, clothing, electronic
assembly, and light consumer durables. It is striking, for example, that, for
goods of these types, production can be set up in "border factories", a labor
force trained, and desired productivity levels achieved in periods of three to
six months in many cases. "Import substitution" in steel, machinery, non-ferrous
metals and other "heavy" industries has much longer gestation and maturation
periods. The scale of activity in the latter type of industries also imposes
greater social dislocations, requires more and quite different technical skills
than traditionally available, and more government services, all with longer
associated delays.

As noted, many aspects of the policy issues which are highlighted by the
foregoing discussions have analogies to the analysis of the optimal amount and
timing of investment in advance of demand for the output of the projects, taking
into account the existence of economies of scale in output. The important
addition to that analysis is consideration of the long lags in the creation of
capacity itself. It is costly to have idle capacity but the extra capacity costs
may be more than justified by the lower costs of output from a large plant, as
demand increases for that output. It is also costly to, first, experience delays
in completing investment projects and then have further delays in achieving rated
productivities because of specific bottlenecks as well as generalized social and

political obstacles. The optimal timing of investment projects involves a balancing of all of these costs.

As an example, returning to the export promotion-import substitution debate, suppose it is intended by country policymakers that import dependence should be reduced in "heavy" industries which have longer delay processes. Nevertheless, it might well be better to take up these industries at a later rather than an earlier stage of overall growth. That would provide time for the country to develop its educational and governmental administrative structures so that these do not contribute to the delays when the heavy industry investment is taken up. The kinds of social adjustment processes which may be of more importance in achieving desired levels of productivity in the heavy industries would also be started but their slow evolution would have less immediate impact if these industries were not at the heart of the growth problem.

This suggestion is, in effect, a guess at the solution to the implicit optimal control problem which characterizes the allocation of resources among sectors and technologies to achieve the goals of development, given all the technological, economic balance and behavioral constraints. It presumes that temporal adjustment processes are, to some extent, separate from the actual development of particular industries. For example, formal education in fields like metallurgy and computer control are distinct from the construction and use of steel mills and computers, though the successful operation of these industries may depend, finally, on the availability of persons with such formal education. Construction of new cities is distinct from the construction of major industrial complexes, although the operation of the latter will depend on the existence of a readily available urban labor force. The extension of the political and administrative structures of government is also distinct from the creation of industries which make important demands for government services.

Yet complete independence does not exist between the supply of educated professionals, an urban labor force and government services and the demands for these conditions for development. Supply decisions will often be made only in response to actual development demands, both by individuals and social including political, institutions. There is unlikely to be complete indifference in the supply reactions to demands of different character. Moreover, some of the conditions for efficient development require experience in an essential way. So the long gestation and maturation lags of particular industries will not be completely avoidable by earlier starts in other industries.

Another example may help make the above, perhaps rather vague reasoning more concrete. The need for managerial and administrative expertise in handling large scale enterprise has already been discussed. To some extent, that expertise can be created through formal training. If one accepts the conventional wisdom, actual experience is also required. If the experience is gained only through full responsibility for a large enterprise, that can be quite expensive in terms of the costs of production. If experience can be gained through management of small enterprise or parts of a larger enterprise, then the final step to large scale management will be easier and presumably the potential risks in taking that final step will be smaller.

This suggests another insight into educational practices and a suggestion. In advanced countries, with large and diversified modern industrial and service sectors, there are many opportunities for on-the-job training and such training is likely to be socially as well as individually less expensive than in less developed countries. If educational practices adjust to these differences there should be relatively more on-the-job training in advanced countries and a greater degree of reliance on formal training in less developed countries. For example, the English educational system appears to be geared to supplying a relatively

high proportion of "generalists" who become specialists through the ample
opportunities for on-the-job training. Yet that may be quite an inappropriate
pattern for developing countries with relatively fewer on-the-job training
opportunities.

An analogous point can be made with respect to the provision of "social
infrastructure". Suppose decisions about the supply of such infrastructure are
based on the patterns observed in advanced countries whose industrial structure
creates relatively heavy demands. That will result in more infrastructure
capacity than needed in developing economies which forego early investment in
industries with heavy infrastructure demands.

With respect to development finance, there are several implications of the
foregoing discussion. There are good reasons for the lesson of experience:
development is a long and often slow process. The rapid growth of the "success"
cases of recent years while suggesting important insights should not lead to the
conclusion that similar trade, investment and pricing policies in other countries
would also lead quickly to the same results. The success cases went through
their own long periods of preparation. They may, as well, have found patterns of
growth which reduced the delay processes. That requires more investigation.

The discussion also emphasizes the intense interdependence in development
among various aspects of the economic and social and political features. This
suggests that, if finance is to be provided on a project-by-project basis, the
temporal structure of influences outside the project which affect its success
must be carefully taken into account, as they may be critical. For program
finance, the different delays in the separate components and, as well, the
temporal processes in the various noneconomic factors will affect the success or
failure of the entire program.

The cliché that there is a great deal of inertia in social systems is suggestive of the long time sequences entailed in many types of economic, social and political change. Some of those are due to delay processes which have their origins in technical factors which are well understood. Other delays are due to less well understood but clearly identifiable processes of change, such as the improvement of judgement with experience. Some of the delays represent the unwillingness of individuals and social groups to modify the patterns of their lives, even defending their traditional patterns against modernization.

The almost total lack of explicit measurements of the various lags and delays in factor supply, in market organization, in political and governmental administrative capabilities and social adjustment processes has been noted frequently above. In view of these inadequacies, is there anything concrete which can be said about the impact of these delay processes on development? Some points which have been made can be summarized: There are delay sequences which are quite long by any standard. These are particularly related to the "non-economic" transformations which must occur in the course of development, but which have a major impact on the effective functioning of the economic system. Those "non-economic" delay sequences also affect the "economic" lags, as examples, the speed with which capital is put in place and the pace at which the labor force learns and adjusts. In an important sense, the social and political transformations are never completed because each step in development imposes new strains on the social and political fabric and calls forth new adaptations.

The lessons of history with respect to the length of these sequences are unsure. That is partly because, for each "successful" country, it is difficult to identify the relative importance of the various constraints on development at any point in time. Each country's unique history and circumstances has conditioned its "response" to the "challenge" of development. Moreover, there have been many changes in the techniques of communication and persuasion over time. So the translation of whatever lessons history may provide into a modern context is a risky enterprise and each observer may come to a somewhat different evaluation.

Undoubtedly it is possible to find unusual individuals and small groups who are thoroughly modernized, even in the least developed countries. The question is about the time period required for the major transformations which permit reasonably full achievement through most of an economy of potential technical productivities. About this, it is only possible to guess. In this author's judgment that period would not, generally, be less than two generations, or, say, fifty years and might well stretch out to twice that time.

It is possible that social and political transformations occur more quickly in small countries because of lower travel and communications costs. "Smallness" often implies relative homogeneity of the society and that can be a characteristic favoring transformation when national leadership is relatively effective. Heterogeneity may facilitate transformation when most of the impetus for change must be generated diffusely within the society. Even if the generalizations are warranted, it is likely that there are exceptions which depend on other characteristics.

There are frequent references to United States as a society in which, "change is built-in," suggesting that the continuing transformations which are required are, in some sense, "easier" than in other countries. This is the kind of generalization which is difficult even to state precisely. The statement can be interpreted to mean that social and political transformations which occur in the early steps in the development process are ones which occur relatively slowly. The U.S. which is, in many ways, a leader in economic "modernization", may find each new step relatively "easy", as compared to the difficulties which face countries in early stages of "modernization," in the sense that the full output potentials of new technologies and institutions are achieved more quickly.

Social transformations are critical in the formation of a modern labor force. The experience and education requirements for professionals and high level managers in the labor force are also exceptionally long and there are interactions among patterns of socialization in the labor force and education and experience sequences. Both processes may go more quickly as development proceeds. Even if the time delays were not shortened, there should be fewer bottlenecks and productivity losses associated with these sequences as development proceeds and more and better opportunities are created for both education and experience. Since the composition of output and the technologies used are likely to be changing relatively rapidly in developing countries, it is still possible that the productivity losses associated with education and experience constraints will be larger in developing than in already developed economies.

The latter statement seems also likely to be characteristic of the constraints associated with new capital formation. The productivity losses which result from "building ahead" are more important at smaller scales of output. The services needed for completing new capital projects and bringing them to their rated outputs quickly are also likely to be scarcer at lower rather than larger output scales.

Again there may be differences between large and small countries. It does not seem to be true that a large country is just a collection of smaller regions each of which can proceed in the same manner as a small country. The center takes away resources from a region and returns those resources but not

necessarily in equal amounts for each region. So some regions which are part of
a larger country will do less well than if developing separately.

The effectiveness of markets will increase with experience. The losses due
to local monopoly power will be lower and the benefits from increased market
participation larger as markets grow and participation increases. How long will
it take for countries to come reasonably close to maximum benefits? No one
knows, but a time scale of decades rather than of a few years appears plausible.

In applying these extremely rough and subjective guesses about the various
time sequences it is necessary to decide when one should "start counting" the
time elapsed. In some respects and for specific features it will be obvious.
The years of education and experience start when education and experience start.
The gestation and maturation periods for new capital projects start when planning
for a project begins and when production begins, respectively. However, it is
necessary to start counting again and again with the temporal sequences through
which each new educational cohort and each investment project must pass.

When do the socialization processes for industrial labor, the organization
of markets and the mobilization of government functions for modernization begin?
The answers, presumably, for nearly every country are both, "a long time ago,"
and, "now." There are few, if any, countries in the world without a history
which has contributed importantly to their modernization and development
processes. For many countries, however, most of what has to be achieved of the
specific conditions necessary for development lies in front of them. Unless
there is excess capacity in infrastructure, labor skills, capacity to provide
government services and easy elasticity in social structures and markets,
continuing economic expansion will require continuing adjustment in all these
dimensions. It is only by examining each country that it is possible to even
hazard a guess about when to, "start counting".

At times in the development process a major set of constraints may be broken or reduced in power and change may accelerate, before subsequently encountering a new set of limitations. While our knowledge of temporal delays created by economic and social constraints is quite limited, it is a greater mistake to ignore them and, in effect, set them at zero, rather than to hazard a conjecture which recognizes and appreciates their existence and significance.

FOOTNOTES

1.   There is a long history of recognition and analysis by economists of lags and temporal sequences in economic activity. The temporal dimension of economics was a central issue to Irving Fisher and the Austrian School, represented by Bohm-Bawerk, for example. For a survey see M. Blaug (1968). It is prominent in the literature on business cycles, especially J.M. Clark (1917, pp. 217-235). Adjustment lags were also treated in the 1920's and 1930's in the early, "cobweb", or "corn-hog" cycle literature to which there were a number of early contributors including P.N. Rosenstein-Rodan (1929). See M. Ezekiel (1938, pp. 255-280) for other citations. They appeared in the economic literature in the modelling of J. Tinbergen (1937) and, to this author's knowledge, were first used in formal models by R. Frisch (1933). This type of business cycle modelling was extended by a number of authors, including P.A. Samuelson (1939, pp. 75-78), Lloyd A. Metzler (1941), and John Hicks (1950).

The incorporation of economic lags in development models was extended from the models of R.F. Harrod (1949) and E.D. Domar (1946, pp. 137-147) by a number of authors including the early work of R. Frisch (1959).

2.   The distinction between maturation and learning-by-doing processes is discussed in R.S. Eckaus (1973).

3.   There was concern with such questions in the earlier stages of discussions of development. A notable, perhaps still unusually rare, example is A. Gerschenkron (1952, pp. 3-30).

4.   Surveying the training literature in 1971, John P. Campbell wrote: "By and large, the training and development literature is voluminous, nonempirical, nontheoretical, poorly written, and dull....it is fadish to an extreme." See Campbell (1971, p. 565). Frank A. Heller and Alfred W. Clark echoed this statement in 1976: "Judging from the paucity of studies reported in the more prestigious journals, training seems to have low status in academia." See Heller and Clark (1976, p. 424). These assessments apparently still reflect the state of the field, as noted in John Van Maanen, (1976, pp. 67-130) and Robin M. Hogarth (1979).

5. A. Gerschenkron, referring mainly to the European and Russian experience in industrialization, as a guide to modern development, writes, "Creation of a labor force that really deserves its name is a most difficult and protracted process." op cit., p.7.

6.   U.S. Department of Labor, Employment and Training Administration, Dictionary of Occupational Titles, 4th edition (Washington Government Printing Office, 1977) and Selected Characteristics of Occupations Defined in the Dictionary of Occupational Titles (Washington Government Printing Office, 1981).

7.   This point was made, for example, by R. Nelson, T.P. Schultz and R.L. Slighton, "The industries where Colombia had developed a relatively large modernized sector by the late 1950's thus tended to be of the routinized, mass production type. Even for such jobs the typical Colombian new employee might require a somewhat longer training period than his better educated American counterpart to reach the same level of effectiveness." (1971, pp. 165-166).

8.   Cf. Neil J. Smelser (1969, pp. 72-90). An empirical study of the changes experienced by British factory workers in their movement from a traditional to a modern work culture is that of John H. Goldthorpe, et al (1968).

9.   In an analysis of migration in Colombia, Gary S. Fields (April 1982, pp. 539-558) found more responsiveness to regional differences in income among individuals with higher levels of educational attainment. Similarly, in a study of Venezuelan migration, T. Paul Schultz (April 1982, pp. 559-593) found that regions of Venezuela with higher levels of primary schooling had higher rates of out-migration. These findings would suggest that more talented individuals are more apt to select to move out of traditional regions and out of traditional roles. See also Simon Kuznets (1969, p. xxxii), Michael J. Hay (January 1980, pp. 345-358) and Jonathon King (October 1978, pp. 83-101).

10. King, op. cit., suggests that Mexican migrants are more apt to migrate to those states in which there is already a large community of individuals who have already migrated from their home-state. Hay, op. cit., found that a Tunisian's decision to migrate was positively related to having a labor-market contact - a relative or friend already living in the urban area to which he was migrating. These findings suggest that the larger groups to which migrants belong facilitate migration. As evidence that the larger groups, especially extended families, benefit from an individual migrant's rewards, A.S. Oberai (March-April 1977, pp. 211-223) found that 44 percent of the members of recent migrants' households were "other relatives," suggesting that members of the extended family join a migrant to benefit from his migration, at least until they are able to find work.

11. For an investigation of these alternatives, see R.S. Eckaus (1973, Ch. 2).

12.   See U.S. Department of Labor, Employment and Training Administration, op.
cit. The educational requirements of various categories of workers in French
manufacturing industries given by Michel Debeauvais (1971, p. 156) is quite
similar to those given by the U.S. Employment and Training Administration.
Presumably training and experience requirements would be perceived to be similar
as well.

In his study of the Brazilian capital goods industry, Nathaniel H. Leff
states:

> According to the sector's foreign company managers, the education
> coefficients noted above, three to four years' schooling for skilled
> workers and five to six years for foremen, are considerably lower than
> those customary in the advanced countries.

To what extent this reflects necessary education, either in Brazil or the
advanced countries, is unclear. Likewise, Leff reports a training and experience
period for Brazilian workers which seems to be shorter than those listed for
similar jobs by the U.S. Employment and Training Administration. Again, however,
it is hard to determine whether the experience and training periods listed for
the United States are in fact necessary.

13.   Cf. Neil J. Smelser, op. cit.; Wilbert E. Moore (1967); Edward B. Harvey
(1975, esp. Ch. 4); Barry A. Turner (1975); Thomas Kutsch (1981, esp. p. 160).
These studies complement the work of Talcott Parsons (1952).

14.   For an eloquent description of the types of social and personal adjustment
necessary in the process of modernization see M.G. Herskovits (1966, pp. 89-
112).

15. Entrepreneurship, which formerly deserved a chapter in development texts, does not even appear in the index of a recent volume. But there is a substantial literature in the 1950's and 1960's, for example, E. Hagen (1962), A.P. Alexander (July 1960, pp. 349-363), C. Geertz (1963). For a recent survey see N. Leff (March 1979, pp. 46-64).

16. Sol Tax, Penny Capitalism, University of Chicago Press, 1953, Theodore W. Schultz, Transforming Traditional Agriculture (New Haven: Yale University Press), 1964, p. 28.

17. Karl Polanyi, The Great Transformation: The Political and Economic Origins of Our Time (New York: Rinehart and Co., 1944).

18. Leonard Binder, et al (1971, esp. pp. 3-72). Of course, political scientists differ in distinguishing and titling these functions. For a discussion of different approaches to the necessary functions which governments must be able to perform as they develop, as well as an attempt at synthesizing them, see Samuel P. Huntington (April 1971, pp. 283-322, esp. p. 312).

19. For a discussion of the economic roles of governments in facilitating economic development, see Joseph J. Spengler (1963, pp. 199-232, esp. pp. 204-206). A comparative historical analysis of the political bases of economic development in Britain, France, Japan and China is provided by Robert T. Holt and John E. Turner (1966, esp. pp. 39-65, 292-33).

20. See Spengler, op. cit., pp. 204-206, Holt and Turner, op. cit., pp. 50-56.

21. Huntington, op. cit., p. 289, in his survey of the political modernization literature, notes that all writers on modernization implicitly or explicitly argue that modernization is a lengthy process. In his own study of political modernization (1983, pp. 13-16), Huntington argues that modernization requires institutionalization of political structures and processes, and that one can be assured that institutionalization has occurred only if a political system has survived at least one generational succession.

22. Huntington, Political Order, p. 34.

23. See Holt and Turner, op. cit., esp. pp. 127-159 on the government's ability to obtain the resources necessary to promote economic development. See also E.V.K. Fitzgerald (1978).

24. Huntington, Political Order, pp. 140-147; Myron Weiner, op. cit., pp. 159-204.

25. Holt and Turner, op. cit., pp. 292-335, study the effects of government actions which stimulate either individual initiative or group action and analyze which of these has been most effective for promoting economic development.

26. One of the features of multisector optimizing models with specific capital which is particularly relevant to this discussion is their explicit treatment of lags in capital formation. This type of modelling could, in principle, be

extended to take into account many of the other types of lags described above. See, for example, R.S. Eckaus and K.S. Parikh (1968), L.M. Goreux (1979), A. Manne (1963).

27. One of the few sources of organized information on gestation periods is T. Mayer (Dec. 22, 1953). It is striking that the lags cited for the various industries more than thirty years ago were seldom as long as three years. Casual empiricism suggests that, in most developing countries, the lags are seldom that short. The "border" or "off-shore" factories being a major exception.

28. The authoritative treatment of these issues is in A. Manne (1966).

29. There are suggestive remarks in R. Nurkse (1953, Ch. 1) and P.N. Rosenstein-Rodan (1943).

BIBLIOGRAPHY

Alexander, A.P. "Industrial Entrepreneurship in Turkey: Origins and Growth,"
    Economic Development and Cultural Change, 8, July 1960, pp. 349-365.

Anderson, C. Arnold, and Mary Jean Bowman, eds. Education and Economic
    Development, Chicago: Aldine Publishing Co., 1965.

Attir, Mustafa O. Burkart Holzner and Zdenek Suda, eds. Directions of Change:
    Modernization Theory, Research, and Realities, Boulder: Westview, 1981.

Berg, Elliot J. "Education and Manpower in Senegal, Guinea, and the Ivory
    Coast." In Frederick Harbison and Charles A. Myers, eds. Manpower and
    Education, New York: McGraw-Hill, 1965.

Bicks, J.S., and C.A. Sinclair. Arab Manpower: The Crisis of Development, New
    York: St. Martin's Press, 1980.

Biersteker, Thomas J. Distortion or Development? Contending Perspectives on the
    Multinational Corporation, Cambridge: MIT Press, 1978.

Binder, Leonard, James S. Coleman, Joseph La Palombara, Lucian W. Pye, Sidney
    Verba, and Myron Weiner. Crises and Sequences in Political Development,
    Princeton: Princeton University Press, 1971.

Blaug, Mark. Economic Theory in Retrospect, 1968.

Blaug, Mark. Education and the Employment Problem in Developing Countries,
    Geneva: ILO, 1973.

Blaug, Mark. "The Unemployment of the Educated in India." In Third World
    Employment: Problems and Strategies, edited by Richard Jolly, Emmanuel De
    Kadt, Hans Singer, and Fiona Wilson. Harmondsworth, England: Penguin,
    1973.

Campbell, John P. "Personnel Training and Development," Annual Review of
    Psychology, 22 (1971): 565-602.

Clark, J.M. "Business Acceleration and the Law of Demand," Journal of Political Economy, XXV, 3, March 1917, pp. 217-235.

Domar, Evsey D. "Capital Expansion, Rate of Growth and Employment," Econometrica, XIV, April 1946, pp. 137-147.

Durand, John D. The Labor Force in Economic Development: A Comparison of International Census Data, 1946-1966, Princeton: Princeton University Press, 1975.

Eckaus, Richard S. "Absorptive Capacity as a Constraint Due to Maturation Processes," in J. Bhagwati and R.S. Eckaus, Development and Planning, London: Allen & Unwin, 1973

Eckaus, Richard S. Estimating the Returns to Education, Carnegie Commission on Higher Education, 1973, Ch. 2.

Eckaus, Richard S. and Kirit S. Parikh. Planning for Growth, Cambridge, Mass.: M.I.T. Press, 1968.

Ezekiel, M. "The Cobweb Theorem," Quarterly Journal of Economics, February 1938, pp. 255-390.

Faunce, William A. and William H. Form, eds. Comparative Perspectives on Industrial Society, Boston: Little, Brown and Co., 1969.

Fields, Gary S. "Place-to-Place Migration in Colombia," Economic Development and Cultural Change, 30, 3 (April 1982), pp. 539-558.

Finkle, Jason R. and Richard W. Gable, eds. Political Development and Social Change, New York: John Wiley and Sons, 1966.

Fitzgerald, E.V.K. "The Fiscal Crisis of the Latin American State." In J.F.J. Toye, ed. Taxation and Economic Development, F. Cass, 1978.

Frank, Isiah. Foreign Enterprise in Developing Countries, Baltimore and London: Johns Hopkins University Press, 1980.

Frisch, R. "A Powerful Method of Approximation in Optimum Investment Computations of the Normal Type," Oslo: University of Oslo Economic Institute, 1959.

Frisch, R. "Propagation Problems and Impulse Problems in Dynamic Economics," Economic Essays in Honor of G. Cassel, London: George Allen and Unwin, 1933.

Geertz, C. Peddlers and Princes, Chicago: U. of Chicago Press, 1963.

Gerschenkron, Alexander. "Economic Backwardness in Historical Perspective," in B. Hoselitz, ed. The Progress of Underdeveloped Areas, Chicago: University of Chicago Press, 1952, pp. 3-30.

Goldthorpe, John H., David Lockwood, Frank Bechhofer, and Jennifer Platt. The Affluent Worker: Industrial Attitudes and Behavior, Cambridge: Cambridge University Press, 1960.

Goreux, L.M. Interdependence in Planning, Baltimore: World Bank and Johns Hopkins U. Press, 1979.

Hagen, Everett E. On the Theory of Social Change, Homewood, Ill.: Dorsey Press, 1962.

Hagen, Everett E. The Economics of Development, 3rd ed., Homewood, Illinois: Irvin, 1980.

Harrod, R.F. Towards A Dynamic Economics, London: Macmillan & Co., 1949.

Harvey, Edward B. Industrial Society: Structures, Roles, and Relations, Homewood, Illinois: Dorsey Press, 1975.

Harbison, Frederick H. Human Resources as the Wealth of Nations, New York: Oxford, 1973.

Harbison, Frederick and Charles A. Myers. Manpower and Education: Country Studies in Economic Development, New York: McGraw-Hill, 1965.

Hay, Michael J. "A Structural Equations Model of Migration in Tunisia," _Economic Development and Cultural Change_, 28, 2 (January 1980): pp. 345-358.

Heller, Frank A. and Alfred W. Clark. "Personnel and Human Resource Development," _Annual Review of Psychology_, 27 (1976): pp. 405-435.

Herskovits, M.J. "The Problem of Adapting Society to New Tasks," in B. Hoselitz, _op. cit._, pp. 89-112.

Hicks, John. _A Contribution to the Theory of the Trade Cycle_, Oxford: Clarendon Press, 1950.

Hirschman, Albert O. _The Strategy of Economic Development_, New Haven: Yale University Press, 1958.

Hirschman, Albert O. _Development Projects Observed_, Washington: Brookings Institution, 1967.

Hogarth, Robin M. _Evaluating Management Education_, New York: John Wiley and Sons, 1979.

Holt, Robert T. and John E. Turner. _The Political Basis of Economic Development: An Exploration in Comparative Political Analysis_, Princeton: D. Van Nostrand Co., 1966.

Horowitz, Morris A. "High-Level Manpower in the Economic Development of Argentina." In Frederick Harbison and Charles A. Myers, eds. _Manpower and Education_, New York: McGraw-Hill, 1965.

Hoselitz, Bert F., and Wilbert E. Moore. _Industrialization and Society_, UNESCO, 1966.

Huntington, Samuel P. _Political Order in Changing Societies_, New Haven: Yale University Press, 1968.

Jolly, Richard, Emmanuel de Kadt, Hans Singer and Fiona Wilson, eds. _Third World Employment: Problems and Strategies_, Harmondsworth, England: Penguin, 1973.

Kindleberger, Charles P. and Bruce Herrick. Economic Development, 3rd ed., New York: McGraw-Hill, 1977.

King, Jonathon. "Interstate Migration in Mexico." Economic Development and Cultural Change, 27, (October 1978): 83-101.

Kutsch, Thomas. "Modernization, Everyday Life, and Social Roles: Benefits and Costs of Life in 'Developed' Societies." In Directions of Change: Modernization Theory, Research, and Realities, edited by Mustafa O. Attir, Burkart Holzner, and Zdenek Suda. Boulder: Westview, 1981.

Kuznets, Simon. "Introduction." In Population Redistribution and Economic Growth, United States, 1870-1950, edited by Hope T. Eldridge and Dorothy Swaine Thomas, Philadephia: American Philosophical Society, 1969.

La Palombara, Joseph, ed. Bureaucracy and Political Development, Princeton: Princeton University Press, 1963.

La Palombara, Joseph and Stephen Blank. Multinational Corporations and Developing Countries, New York: The Conference Board, 1979.

Leff, Nathaniel H. Economic Policy-Making and Development in Brazil, 1947-1964, New York: John Wiley and Sons, 1968.

Leff, Nathaniel H. The Brazilian Capital Goods Industry, 1929-1964, Cambridge: Harvard University Press, 1960.

Leff Nathaniel H. "Entrepreneurship and Development," Journal of Economic Literature, XVII, 1, March, 1979, pp. 46-64.

Lengyel, Peter, ed. Approaches to the Science of Socio-economic Development, Paris: UNESCO, 1971.

Loehr, William, and John P. Powelson. The Economics of Development and Distribution, New York: Harcourt Brace Jovanovich, 1981.

Maddison, Angus. Foreign Skills and Technical Assistance in Economic Development Paris: OECD, 1966.

Meier, Gerald M. Leading Issues in Economic Development: Studies in
    International Poverty, 2nd ed. Oxford, New York, 1970.

Manne, A. Investment for Capacity Expansion, London: Allen & Unwin, 1966.

Manne, A. "Key Sectors of the Mexican Economy," in A. Manne and H. Markowitz,
    Studies in Process Analysis, New York: John Wiley & Sons, 1963.

Mayer, T. "Input Lead Times for Capital Coefficients," Bureau of Mines, Office
    of Chief Economist, Interindustry Research. Item No. 52, Dec. 22, 1953.

Metzler, Lloyd A. "The Nature and Stability of Inventory Cycles," The Review of
    Economics and Statistics, XXIII, August 1941.

Masannat, George S., ed. The Dynamics of Modernization of Social Change, Pacific
    Palisades, California: Goodyear Publishing Co., 1973.

Moore, Wilbert E. Industrialization and Labor: Social Aspects of Economic
    Development, New York: Russell and Russell, 1965.

Moore, Wilbert E. Order and Change: Essays in Comparative Sociology, New York:
    John Wiley and Sons, 1967.

Moore, Wilbert E. "Changes in Occupational Structures." In William A. Faunce
    and William H. Form, eds. Comparative Perspectives on Industrial Society,
    Boston: Little, Brown, and Co., 1969.

Musgrave, Richard A. "Notes on Educational Investment in Developing Nations."
    In Gerald M. Maier, ed. Leading Issues in Economic Development, 2nd ed.
    New York: Oxford University Press, 1970.

Myrdal, Gunnar. "The Effect of Education on Attitudes to Work." In Third World
    Employment: Problems and Strategies, edited by Richard Jolly, Emmanuel De
    Kadt, Hans Singer, and Fiona Wilson. Harmondsworth, England: Penguin,
    1973.

Nelson, R., T.P. Schultz and R.L. Slighton. Structural Change in a Developing
    Economy, Princeton: Princeton U. Press, 1971.

Ness, Gayl D., ed. The Sociology of Economic Development, New York: Harper and Row, 1970.

Nurkse, R. Problems of Capital Formation in Underdeveloped Countries, New York: Oxford U. Press, 1953, Ch. 1.

Oberai, A.S. "Migration, Unemployment and the Urban Labour Market: A Case Study of the Sudan," International Labour Review, 115, 2 (March-April, 1977): 211-223.

Organski, A.F.K. The Stages of Political Development, New York: Alfred A. Knopf, 1965.

Ranis, Gustav, ed. Government and Economic Development, New Haven: Yale University Press, 1971.

Rosenstein-Rodan, P.N. "Das Zeitmoment in der Mathematischen Theorie des Wirtsch Gleichgewichtes" ("The Role of Time in Economic Theory") Zeitschrift F. Nationalokonomie, 1929.

Rosenstein-Rodan, P.N. "Problems of the Industrialization of Eastern and Southeastern Europe," Economic Journal, 1943.

Samuelson, Paul A. "Interactions Between The Multiplier Analysis and The Principle of Acceleration," The Review of Economics and Statistics, XXI, 2, May 1939, pp. 75-78.

Schultz, T. Paul, "Lifetime Migration within Educational Strata in Venezuela: Estimates of a Logistic Model," Economic Development and Cultural Change, 30, 3 (April 1982): pp. 559-593.

Schultz, Theodore W. Transforming Traditional Agriculture, New Haven: Yale U. Press, 1964, p. 28.

Selzer, George "High-Level Manpower in Nyasaland Development." In Frederick Harbison and Charles A. Myers, eds. Manpower and Education, New York: McGraw-Hill, 1965.

Smelser, Neil J. The Sociology of Economic Life, 2nd ed., Englewood Cliffs, New
    Jersey: Prentice-Hall, 1976.

Smelser, Neil J. "Mechanisms of Change and Adjustment to Change." In William A.
    Faunce and William H. Form, eds. Comparative Perspectives on Industrial
    Society, Boston: Little, Brown, and Co., 1969.

Spengler, Joseph J. "Bureaucracy and Economic Development." In Joseph La
    Palombara, ed. Bureaucracy and Political Development, Princeton: Princeton
    University Press.

Staley, Eugene. "The Role of the State in Economic Development." In Myron
    Weiner, ed. Modernization, New York: Basic Books, 1966.

Tax, Sol. Penny Capitalism, Chicago: U. of Chicago Press, 1953.

Thomas, Brinley. Migration and Economic Growth: A Study of Great Britain and
    the Atlantic Economy, 2nd ed., Cambridge: Cambridge University Press, 1973.

Tinbergen, J. An Econometric Approach to Business Cycle Problems, Paris, 1937.

Turner, Barry A. Industrialism, London: Longman, 1975.

Van Maanen, John. "Breaking In: Socialization to Work." In Robert Dubin, ed.
    Handbook of Work, Organization, and Society, Chicago: Rand McNally, 1976.

Waldo, Dwight, ed. Temporal Dimensions of Development Administration, Durham,
    North Carolina: Duke University Press, 1970.

Weiner, Myron, ed. Modernization, New York: Basic Books, 1966.

Whyte, William Foote, with the collaboration of Graciela Flores. "High-Level
    Manpower for Peru." In Frederick Harbison and Charles A. Myers, eds.
    Manpower and Education, New York: McGraw-Hill, 1965.

World Bank Publications of Related Interest

Accelerated Development in Sub-Saharan Africa: An Agenda for Action

In the fall of 1979, the African Governors of the World Bank addressed a memorandum to the Bank's president expressing their alarm at the dim economic prospects for the nations of sub-Saharan Africa and asking that the Bank prepare a "special paper on the economic development problems of these countries" and an appropriate program for helping them. This report, building on the *Lagos Plan of Action*, is the response to that request.

The report discusses the factors that explain slow economic growth in Africa in the recent past, analyzes policy changes and program orientations needed to promote faster growth, and concludes with a set of recommendations to donors, including the recommendation that aid to Africa should double in real terms to bring about renewed African development and growth in the 1980s. The report's agenda for action is general; it indicates broad policy and program directions, overall priorities for action, and key areas for donor attention. Like the *Lagos Plan*, the report recognizes that Africa has enormous economic potential, which awaits fuller development.

1981; 2nd printing 1982. 198 pages (including statistical annex, bibliography).

French: Le développement accéléré en afrique au sud du Sahara: programme indicatif d'action.
Stock Nos. SA-1981-E, SA-1981-F. Free of charge.

The Design of Development
Jan Tinbergen

Formulates a coherent government policy to further development objectives and outlines methods to stimulate private investments.

The Johns Hopkins University Press, 1958; 6th printing, 1966. 108 pages (including 4 annexes, index).
LC 58-9458. ISBN 0-8018-0633-X, $5.00 (£3.00) paperback.

Development Strategies in Semi-Industrial Economies
Bela Balassa

Provides an analysis of development strategies in semi-industrial economies that have established an industrial base. Endeavors to quantify the systems of incentives that are applied in six semi-industrial developing economies—Argentina, Colombia, Israel, Korea, Singapore, and Taiwan—and to indicate the effects of these systems on the allocation of resources, international trade, and economic growth.

The Johns Hopkins University Press, 1982. 416 pages (including appendixes, index).
LC 81-15558. ISBN 0-8018-2569-5, $39.95 hardcover.

Eastern and Southern Africa: Past Trends and Future Prospects
Ravi Gulhati

World Bank Staff Working Paper No. 413. August 1980. 24 pages.
Stock No. WP-0413. $3.00.

Economic Development Projects and Their Appraisal: Cases and Principles from the Experience of the World Bank
John A. King

The English-language edition is out of print.

French: Projets de développement économique et leur évaluation. *Dunod Editeur, 24–26, boulevard de l'Hôpital, 75005 Paris, France. 1969.*
99 francs.
Spanish: La evaluacion de proyectors de desarrollo económico. *Editorial Tecnos, 1970. 545 pages (including indexes).*
800 pesetas.

Economic Growth and Human Resources
Norman Hicks, assisted by Jahangir Boroumand

World Bank Staff Working Paper No. 408. July 1980. iv + 36 pages (including 3 appendixes, bibliography, and references).
Stock No. WP-0408. $3.00.

NEW

The Extent of Poverty in Latin America
Oscar Altimir

This work originated in a research project for the measurement and analysis of income distribution in the Latin American countries, undertaken jointly by the Economic Commission for Latin America and the World Bank. Presents estimates of the extent of absolute poverty for ten Latin American countries and for the region as a whole in the 1970s.

World Bank Staff Working Paper No. 522. 1982. 117 pages.
ISBN 0-8213-0012-1. $5.00.

First Things First: Meeting Basic Human Needs in the Developing Countries
Paul Streeten, with
Shahid Javed Burki,
Mahbub ul Haq,
Norman Hicks,
and Frances Stewart

The basic needs approach to economic development is one way of helping the poor emerge from their poverty. It enables them to earn or obtain the necessities for life—nutrition, housing, water and sanitation, education, and health—and thus to increase their productivity.

This book answers the critics of the basic needs approach, views this approach as a logical step in the evolution of economic analysis and development policy, and presents a clearsighted interpretation of the issues. Based on the actual experience of various countries—their successes and failures—the book is a distillation of World Bank studies of the operational implications of meeting basic needs. It also discusses the presumed conflict between economic growth and basic needs, the relation between the New International Economic Order and basic needs, and the relation between human rights and basic needs.

Oxford University Press, 1981; 2nd paperback printing, 1982. 224 pages (including appendix, bibliography, index).

LC 81-16836, ISBN 0-19-520-368-2, $18.95 hardcover; ISBN 0-19-520-369-0, $7.95 paperback.

The Hungarian Economic Reform, 1968–81
Bela Balassa

Reviews the Hungarian experience with the economic reform introduced in 1968 and provides a short description of the antecedents of the reform. Analyzes specific reform measures concerning agriculture, decisionmaking by industrial firms, price determination, the exchange rate, export subsidies, import protection, and investment decisions and indicates their effects on the economy. Also examines the economic effects of tendencies toward recentralization in the 1970s, as well as recent policy measures aimed at reversing these tendencies.

World Bank Staff Working Paper No. 506. February 1982. 31 pages (including references).

Stock No. WP-0506. $3.00.

Implementing Programs of Human Development
Edited by Peter T. Knight; prepared by Nat J. Colletta, Jacob Meerman, and others.

World Bank Staff Working Paper No. 403. July 1980. iv + 372 pages (including references).

Stock No. WP-0403. $15.00.

International Technology Transfer: Issues and Policy Options
Frances Stewart

World Bank Staff Working Paper No. 344. July 1979. xii + 166 pages (including references).

Stock No. WP-0344. $5.00.

Levels of Poverty: Policy and Change
Amartya Sen

World Bank Staff Working Paper No. 401. July 1980. 91 pages (including references).

Stock No. WP-0401. $3.00.

Models of Growth and Distribution for Brazil
Lance Taylor, Edmar L. Bacha, Eliana Cardoso, and Frank J. Lysy

Explores the Brazilian experience from the point of view of political economy and computable general equilibrium income distribution models.

Oxford University Press, 1980. 368 pages (including references, appendixes, index).

LC 80-13786. ISBN 0-19-520206-6, $27.50 hardcover; ISBN 0-19-520207-4, $14.95 paperback.

Four chapters provide an overview of alternative strategies; a detailed look at health, education, nutrition, and fertility; lessons from existing programs; and an examination of broader issues in planning.

Oxford University Press. 1982. 96 pages (including statistical appendix).

LC 82-2153. ISBN 0-19-520389-5, $7.95 paperback.

Reforming the New Economic Mechanism in Hungary
Bela Balassa

Evaluates the reform measures taken in 1980 and 1981 (price setting, the exchange rate and protection, wage determination and personal incomes, investment decisions, and the organizational structure) that aim at the further development of the Hungarian New Economic Mechanism, introduced on January 1, 1968.

World Bank Staff Working Paper No. 534. 1982. 56 pages.

ISBN 0-8213-0048-2. $3.00.

Social Infrastructure and Services in Zimbabwe
Rashid Faruqee

The black majority government of Zimbabwe, coming to power after a long struggle for independence, has announced its strong commitment to social services to benefit the vast majority of the population. This paper looks at issues related to education, health, housing, and other important sectors and reviews specific plans and resource requirements to help improve the standard of living of the population.

World Bank Staff Working Paper No. 495. October 1981. 111 pages (including bibliography, map).

Stock No. WP-0495. $5.00.

Structural Change and Development Policy
Hollis Chenery

A retrospective look at Chenery's thought and writing over the past two decades and an extension of his work in *Redistribution with Growth* and *Patterns of Development.* Develops a set of techniques for analyzing structural changes and applies them to some major problems of developing countries today.

Oxford University Press, 1979; 2nd paperback printing, 1982. 544 pages (including references, index).

LC 79-18026. ISBN 0-19-520094-2, $34.50 hardcover; ISBN 0-19-520095-0, $12.95 paperback.

French: Changement des structures et politique de développement. *Economica, 1981.*

ISBN 2-7178-0404-8, 80 francs.

Spanish: Cambio estructural y política de desarrollo. *Editorial Tecnos, 1980.*

ISBN 84-309-0845-5, 1,000 pesetas.

Tourism—Passport to Development? Perspectives on the Social and Cultural Effects of Tourism in Developing Countries
Emanuel de Kadt, editor

The first serious effort at dealing with the effects of tourism development in a broad sense, concentrating on social and cultural questions.

A joint World Bank–Unesco study. Oxford University Press, 1979. 378 pages (including maps, index).

LC 79-18116. ISBN 0-19-520149-3, $24.95 hardcover; ISBN 0-19-520150-7, $9.95 paperback.

French: Le tourisme—passport pour le développement: regards sur les effets socioculturels du tourisme dans les pays en voie de développement. Economica, 1980.

49 francs.

Tribal Peoples and Economic Development: Human Ecologic Considerations
Robert Goodland

At the current time, approximately 200 million tribal people live in all regions of the world and number among the poorest of the poor. This paper describes the problems associated with the development process as it affects tribal peoples; it outlines the requisites for meeting the human ecologic needs of tribal peoples; and presents general principles that are designed to assist the Banks staff and project designers in incorporating appropriate procedures to ensure the survival of tribal peoples and to assist with their development.

May 1982, vii + 111 pages (including 7 annexes, bibliography).

ISBN 0-8213-0010-5. $5.00.

The Tropics and Economic Development: A Provocative Inquiry into the Poverty of Nations
Andrew M. Kamarck

Examines major characteristics of the tropical climates that are significant to economic development.

The Johns Hopkins University Press, 1976; 2nd printing, 1979. 128 pages (including maps, bibliography, index).

LC 76-17242. ISBN 0-8018-1891-5, $11.00 (£7.75) hardcover; ISBN 0-8018-1903-2, $5.00 (£3.50) paperback.

French: Les tropiques et le développement économique: un regard sans complaisance sur la pauvreté des nations. *Economica, 1978.*

ISBN 2-7178-0110-3, 25 francs.

Spanish: Los trópicos y desarrollo económico: reflexiones sobre la pobreza de las naciones. *Editorial Tecnos, 1978.*

ISBN 84-309-0740-8, 350 pesetas.

Twenty-five Years of Economic Development, 1950 to 1975
David Morawetz

A broad assessment of development efforts shows that, although the developing countries have been

Patterns of Development, 1950-1970
Hollis Chenery
and Moises Syrquin

A comprehensive interpretation of the structural changes that accompany the growth of developing countries, using cross-section and time-series analysis to study the stability of observed patterns and the nature of time trends.

Oxford University Press, 1975; 3rd paperback printing, 1980. 250 pages (including technical appendix, statistical appendix, bibliography, index).

LC 74-29172. ISBN 0-19-920075-0, $19.95 hardcover; ISBN 0-19-920076-9, $8.95 paperback.

Spanish: La estructura del crecimiento ecónomico: un analisis para el período 1950–1970. Editorial Teconos, 1978.

ISBN 84-309-0741-6, 615 pesetas.

Poverty and Basic Needs Series

A series of booklets prepared by the staff of the World Bank on the subject of basic needs. The series includes general studies that explore the concept of basic needs, country case studies, and sectoral studies.

Brazil
Peter T. Knight and
Ricardo J. Moran

An edited and updated edition of the more detailed publication, *Brazil: Human Resources Special Report* (see description under *Country Studies* listing).

December 1981. 98 pages (including statistical appendix, map). English.

Stock No. BN-8103. $5.00.

Malnourished People: A Policy View
Alan Berg

Discusses the importance of adequate nutrition as an objective, as well as a means of economic development. Outlines the many facets of the nutrition problem and shows how efforts to improve nutrition can help alleviate much of the human and economic waste in the developing world.

June 1981. 108 pages (including 6 appendixes, notes). English. French and Spanish (forthcoming).

Stock Nos. BN-8104-E, BN-8104-F, BN-8104-S. $5.00.

Meeting Basic Needs: An Overview
Mahbub ul Haq and
Shahid Javed Burki

Presents a summary of the main findings of studies undertaken in the World Bank as part of a program for reducing absolute poverty and meeting basic needs.

September 1980. 28 pages (including 2 annexes). English, French, Spanish, Japanese, and Arabic.

Stock Nos. BN-8001-E, BN-8001-F, BN-8001-S, BN-8001-J, BN-8001-A. $3.00 paperback.

Shelter
Anthony A. Churchill

Defines the elements that constitute shelter; discusses the difficulties encountered in developing shelter programs for the poor; estimates orders of magnitude of shelter needs for the next twenty years; and proposes a strategy for meeting those needs.

September 1980. 39 pages. English, French, and Spanish.

Stock Nos. BN-8002-E, BN-8002-F, BN-8002-S. $3.00 paperback.

Water Supply and Waste Disposal

Discusses the size of the problem of meeting basic needs in water supply and waste disposal and its significance to development in the context of the International Drinking Water Supply and Sanitation Decade. Examines the Bank's past role in improving water supply and waste disposal facilities in developing countries and draws conclusions for the future.

September 1980. 46 pages. English, French, Spanish, and Arabic.

Stock Nos. BN-8003-E, BN-8003-F, BN-8003-S, BN-8003-A. $3.00 paperback.

Poverty and the Development of Human Resources: Regional Perspective
Willem Bussink, David Davies, Roger Grawe, Basil Kavalsky, and Guy P. Pfeffermann

World Bank Staff Working Paper No. 406. July 1980. iii + 197 pages (including 7 tables, 2 appendixes, references, footnotes).

Stock No. WP-0406. $5.00.

NEW

Poverty and Human Development
Paul Isenman and others

Since economic growth alone has r reduced absolute poverty, it has be necessary to consider other strategies. The strategy examined i this study — human development - epitomizes the idea that poor peop should be helped to help themselv remarkably successful in achieving growth, the distribution of its benefits among and within countries has been less satisfactory.

The Johns Hopkins University Press, 1977; 3rd printing, 1981. 136 pages (including statistical appendix, references).

LC 77-17243. ISBN 0-8018-2134-7, $16.50 (£8.00) hardcover; ISBN 0-8018-2092-8, $7.95 (£3.75) paperback.

French: Vingt-cinq années de développement économique: 1950 à 1975. *Economica, 1978.*

ISBN 2-7178-0038-7, 26 francs.

Spanish: Veinticinco años de desarrollo económico: 1950 a 1975. *Editorial Tecnos, 1978.*

ISBN 84-309-0792-0, 350 pesetas.

World Development Report

A large-format series of annual studies of about 200 pages, the *World Development Report,* since its inception, has been what *The Guardian* has called "a most remarkable publication. It is the nearest thing to having an annual report on the present state of the planet and the people who live on it." Each issue brings not only an overview of the state of development, but also a detailed analysis of such topics as structural change, the varying experiences of low- and middle-income countries, the relation of poverty and human resource development, global and national adjustment, and agriculture and food stability. Each contains a statistical annex, World Development Indicators, that provides profiles of more than 120 countries in twenty-five multipage tables. The data cover such subjects as demography, industry, trade, energy, finance, and development assistance and such measures of social conditions as education, health, and nutrition.

World Development Report 1982
(See Publications of Particular Interest for description and sales information.)

World Development Report 1981
(Discusses adjustment—global and national—to promote sustainable growth in the changing world economy.)

World Development Report 1980
(Discusses adjustment and growth in the 1980s and poverty and human development.)

World Development Report 1979
(Discusses development prospects and international policy issues, structural change, and country development experience and issues.)

World Development Report 1978
(Disusses the development experience, 1950–75, development priorities in the middle-income developing countries, and prospects for alleviating poverty.)

REPRINTS

Basic Needs: The Case of Sri Lanka
Paul Isenman

World Bank Reprint Series: Number 197. Reprinted from World Development. *vol. 8 (1980): 237-58.*

Stock No. RP-0197. Free of charge.

Brazilian Socioeconomic Development: Issues for the Eighties
Peter T. Knight

World Bank Reprint Series: Number 203. Reprinted from World Development. *vol. 9, no. 11/12 (1981):1063-82.*

Stock No. RP-0203. Free of charge.

Indigenous Anthropologists and Development-Oriented Research
Michael M. Cernea

World Bank Reprint Series: Number 208. Reprinted from Indigenous Anthropology in Non-Western Countries. *edited by Hussein Fahim (Durham, North Carolina: Carolina Academic Press, 1982):121-37.*

Stock No. RP-0208. Free of charge.

Latin America and the Caribbean: Economic Performance and Policies
Guy P. Pfeffermann

World Bank Reprint Series: Number 228. Reprinted from The Southwestern Review of Management and Economics. *vol. 2, no. 1 (Winter 1982):129-72.*
Stock No. RP-0228. Free of charge.

Modernization and Development Potential of Traditional Grass Roots Peasant Organizations
Michael M. Cernea

World Bank Reprint Series: Number 215. Reprinted from Directions of Change: Modernization Theory, Research, and Realities. *Boulder, Colorado: Westview Press (1981): chapter 5.*
Stock No. RP-0215. Free of charge.

WORLD BANK PUBLICATIONS
ORDER FORM

SEND TO:

WORLD BANK PUBLICATIONS **P.O. BOX 37525** **WASHINGTON, D.C. 20013** **U.S.A.**	**or**	**WORLD BANK PUBLICATIONS** **66, AVENUE D'IÉNA** **75116 PARIS, FRANCE**

Name: _____

Address: _____

_____

Stock or ISBN #	Author, Title	Qty.	Price	Total

Sub-Total Cost: _____

Postage & handling fee for more than two free items ($1.00 each): _____

Total copies: _____ Air mail surcharge ($2.00 each): _____

TOTAL PAYMENT ENCLOSED: _____

Make checks payable: WORLD BANK PUBLICATIONS

Prepayment on orders from individuals is requested. Purchase orders are accepted from booksellers, library suppliers, libraries, and institutions. All prices include cost of postage by the least expensive means. The prices and publication dates quoted in this Catalog are subject to change without notice.

No refunds will be given for items that cannot be filled. Credit will be applied towards future orders.

No more than two free publications will be provided without charge. Requests for additional copies will be filled at a charge of US $1.00 per copy to cover handling and postage costs.

Airmail delivery will require a prepayment of US $2.00 per copy.

Mail-order payment to the World Bank need not be in U.S. dollars, but the amount remitted must be at the rate of exchange on the day the order is placed. The World Bank will also accept Unesco coupons.